Presented to:

Never Forget The Difference You've Made

Made in United States
North Haven, CT
02 December 2021

11858009R00065